The Essential Buyer's Guide

Mercedes-Benz

SL

R129-series 1989-2001

Your marque expert:
Julian Parish

T0386362

VELOCE PUBLISHING
THE PUBLISHER OF FINE AUTOMOTIVE BOOKS

Alfa Romeo Alfasud (Metcalfe)
Alfa Romeo Alfetta: all saloon/sedan models 1972 to 1984 & coupé models 1974 to 1987 (Metcalfe)
Alfa Romeo Giulia GT Coupé (Booker)
Alfa Romeo Giulia Spider (Booker)
Audi TT (Davies)
Audi TT Mk2 2006 to 2014 (Durnan)
Austin-Healey Big Healeys (Trummel)
BMW Boxer Twins (Henshaw)
BMW E30 3 Series 1981 to 1994 (Hosier)
BMW GS (Henshaw)
BMW X5 (Saunders)
BMW Z3 Roadster (Fishwick)
BMW Z4: E85 Roadster and E86 Coupé including M and Alpina 2003 to 2009 (Smitheram)
BSA 350, 441 & 500 Singles (Henshaw)
BSA 500 & 650 Twins (Henshaw)
BSA Bantam (Henshaw)
Choosing, Using & Maintaining Your Electric Bicycle (Henshaw)
Citroën 2CV (Paxton)
Citroën DS & ID (Heilig)
Cobra Replicas (Ayre)
Corvette C2 Sting Ray 1963-1967 (Falconer)
Datsun 240Z 1969 to 1973 (Newlyn)
DeLorean DMC-12 1981 to 1983 (Williams)
Ducati Bevel Twins (Falloon)
Ducati Desmodue Twins (Falloon)
Ducati Desmoquattro Twins – 851, 888, 916, 996, 998, ST4 1988 to 2004 (Falloon)
FIAT 124 Spider & Pininfarina Azzura Spider, (AS-DS) 1966 to 1985 (Robertson)
Fiat 500 & 600 (Bobbitt)
Ford Capri (Paxton)
Ford Escort Mk1 & Mk2 (Williamson)
Ford Focus Mk1 RS & ST170, 1st Generation (Williamson)
Ford Model A – All Models 1927 to 1931 (Buckley)
Ford Model T – All models 1909 to 1927 (Barker)
Ford Mustang – First Generation 1964 to 1973 (Cook)
Ford Mustang – 3rd generation: 1979-1993; inc Mercury Capri: 1979-1986 (Smith)

Ford Mustang – Fifth Generation (2005-2014) (Cook)
Ford RS Cosworth Sierra & Escort (Williamson)
Harley-Davidson Big Twins (Henshaw)
Hillman Imp (Morgan)
Hinckley Triumph triples & fours 750, 900, 955, 1000, 1050, 1200 – 1991-2009 (Henshaw)
Honda CBR FireBlade (Henshaw)
Honda CBR600 Hurricane (Henshaw)
Honda SOHC Fours 1969-1984 (Henshaw)
Jaguar E-Type 3.8 & 4.2 litre (Crespin)
Jaguar E-type V12 5.3 litre (Crespin)
Jaguar Mark 1 & 2 (All models including Daimler 2.5-litre V8) 1955 to 1969 (Thorley)
Jaguar New XK 2005-2014 (Thorley)
Jaguar S-Type – 1999 to 2007 (Thorley)
Jaguar X-Type – 2001 to 2009 (Thorley)
Jaguar XJ-S (Crespin)
Jaguar XJ6, XJ8 & XJR (Thorley)
Jaguar XK 120, 140 & 150 (Thorley)
Jaguar XK8 & XKR (1996-2005) (Thorley)
Jaguar/Daimler XJ 1994-2003 (Crespin)
Jaguar/Daimler XJ40 (Crespin)
Jaguar/Daimler XJ6, XJ12 & Sovereign (Crespin)
Kawasaki Z1 & Z900 (Orritt)
Lancia Delta HF 4WD & Integrale (Baker)
Land Rover Discovery Series 1 (1989-1998) (Taylor)
Land Rover Discovery Series 2 (1998-2004) (Taylor)
Land Rover Series I, II & IIA (Thurman)
Land Rover Series III (Thurman)
Lotus Elan, S1 to Sprint and Plus 2 to Plus 2S 130/5 1962 to 1974 (Vale)
Lotus Europa, S1, S2, Twin-cam & Special 1966 to 1975 (Vale)
Lotus Seven replicas & Caterham 7: 1973-2013 (Hawkins)
Mazda MX-5 Miata (Mk1 1989-97 & Mk2 98-2001) (Crook)
Mazda MX-5 Miata (Mk3, 3.5 &

3.75 models, 2005-2015) (Wild)
Mazda RX-8 (Parish)
Mercedes-Benz 190: all 190 models (W201 series) 1982 to 1993 (Parish)
Mercedes-Benz 280-560SL & SLC (Bass)
Mercedes-Benz G-Wagen (Greene)
Mercedes-Benz Pagoda 230SL, 250SL & 280SL roadsters & coupés (Bass)
Mercedes-Benz S-Class W126 Series (Zoporowski)
Mercedes-Benz S-Class Second Generation W116 Series (Parish)
Mercedes-Benz SL R129-series 1989 to 2001 (Parish)
Mercedes-Benz SLK (Bass)
Mercedes-Benz W123 (Parish)
Mercedes-Benz W124 – All models 1984-1997 (Zoporowski)
MG Midget & A-H Sprite (Horler)
MG TD, TF & TF1500 (Jones)
MGA 1955-1962 (Crosier)
MGB & MGB GT (Williams)
MGF & MG TF (Hawkins)
Mini (Paxton)
Morgan 4/4 (Benfield)
Morgan Plus 4 (Benfield)
Morris Minor & 1000 (Newell)
Moto Guzzi 2-valve big twins (Falloon)
New Mini (Collins)
Norton Commando (Henshaw)
Peugeot 205 GTI (Blackburn)
Piaggio Scooters – all modern two-stroke & four-stroke automatic models 1991 to 2016 (Willis)
Porsche 356 (Johnson)
Porsche 911 (964) (Streather)
Porsche 911 (991) (Streather)
Porsche 911 (993) (Streather)
Porsche 911 (996) (Streather)
Porsche 911 (997) – Model years 2004 to 2009 (Streather)
Porsche 911 (997) – Second generation models 2009 to 2012 (Streather)
Porsche 911 Carrera 3.2 (Streather)
Porsche 911SC (Streather)
Porsche 924 – All models 1976 to 1988 (Hodgkins)
Porsche 928 (Hemmings)
Porsche 930 Turbo & 911 (930) Turbo (Streather)
Porsche 944 (Higgins)

Porsche 981 Boxster & Cayman (Streather)
Porsche 986 Boxster (Streather)
Porsche 987 Boxster and Cayman 1st generation (2005-2009) (Streather)
Porsche 987 Boxster and Cayman 2nd generation (2009-2012) (Streather)
Range Rover – First Generation models 1970 to 1996 (Taylor)
Range Rover – Second Generation 1994-2001 (Taylor)
Range Rover – Third Generation L322 (2002-2012) (Taylor)
Reliant Scimitar GTE (Payne)
Rolls-Royce Silver Shadow & Bentley T-Series (Bobbitt)
Rover 2000, 2200 & 3500 (Marrocco)
Royal Enfield Bullet (Henshaw)
Subaru Impreza (Hobbs)
Sunbeam Alpine (Barker)
Triumph 350 & 500 Twins (Henshaw)
Triumph Bonneville (Henshaw)
Triumph Herald & Vitesse (Ayre)
Triumph Spitfire and GT6 (Ayre)
Triumph Stag (Mort)
Triumph Thunderbird, Trophy & Tiger (Henshaw)
Triumph TR2 & TR3 - All models (including 3A & 3B) 1953 to 1962 (Conners)
Triumph TR4/4A & TR5/250 - All models 1961 to 1968 (Child & Battyll)
Triumph TR6 (Williams)
Triumph TR7 & TR8 (Williams)
Triumph Trident & BSA Rocket III (Rooke)
TVR Chimaera and Griffith (Kitchen)
TVR S-series (Kitchen)
Velocette 350 & 500 Singles 1946 to 1970 (Henshaw)
Vespa Scooters – Classic 2-stroke models 1960-2008 (Paxton)
Volkswagen Bus (Copping)
Volkswagen Transporter T4 (1990-2003) (Copping/Cservenka)
VW Golf GTI (Copping)
VW Beetle (Copping)
Volvo 700/900 Series (Beavis)
Volvo P1800/1800S, E & ES 1961 to 1973 (Murray)

www.veloce.co.uk

First published in November 2016, reprinted April 2022 by Veloce Publishing Limited, Veloce House, Parkway Farm Business Park, Middle Farm Way, Poundbury, Dorchester, Dorset, DT1 3AR, England.
Fax 01305 250479/e-mail info@veloce.co.uk/web www.veloce.co.uk or www.velocebooks.com.
ISBN: 978-1-845848-98-9 UPC: 6-36847-04898-3
Readers with ideas for automotive books, or books on other transport or related hobby subjects, are invited to write to the editorial director of Veloce Publishing at the above address.
British Library Cataloguing in Publication Data – A catalogue record for this book is available from the British Library.
Typesetting, design and page make-up all by Veloce Publishing Ltd on Apple Mac.
Printed and bound by CPI Group (UK) Ltd, Croydon, CR0 4YY.

When Mercedes-Benz presented the R129-series SL at the Geneva Motor Show in 1989, it was eagerly awaited: its predecessor, the R107, had been in production for 18 years. During the intervening years, Mercedes' engineers had been busy launching models like the compact 190 saloon (W201) with many new features. The R129 marked a major change, which unsettled some traditionalists. But Mercedes

Princess Diana's 500SL on show at the Mercedes Museum in Stuttgart.

need not have worried: the latest SL was an immediate success, with waiting lists stretching to five years and celebrity owners including Princess Diana. Over its 12-year career, more than 200,000 cars would be sold.

At nearly 1800kg (4000lb) for the SL500, the R129 gave the lie to its *Sport Leicht* (or *Sport Light*) name. Setting aside the AMG models, it is probably best regarded as an outstanding Grand Tourer or 'personal luxury car' rather than an outright sports car.

The R129 represented a huge advance in engineering terms. A sophisticated new suspension was fitted to all models and – for the first time on an SL – a V12 engine and five-speed automatic transmission became available. Extensive use of light alloys and high-strength steels ensured that torsional strength was improved by 30% over the R107, while the drag coefficient (with the hardtop on) was slashed from 0.44 to 0.32. Many safety features were introduced, including an automatic roll-over bar (which deployed in just 0.3 seconds in an emergency), integrated front seat belts, anti-lock brakes (ABS) and traction control system (ASR).

Today, the R129 is increasingly accepted as a modern classic. Bruno Sacco's effortlessly elegant styling has aged well, and the R129 feels much more modern to drive than the

Mechanism of automatic roll-over bar shows the complexity of the R129's systems.
(Courtesy Mercedes-Benz Classic)

R107. The last SL with a separate, removable hardtop, it has the outstanding build quality typical of Mercedes' cars of the era, markedly superior to that of the R230 which followed. Although generally reliable, it is a complex car, with far more use of electronic and hydraulic systems. The folding soft top alone requires 15 pressure cylinders. Prices of the earlier 190SL, 'Pagoda' and R107 SLs have already risen sharply, and those of the R129 are now starting to move up. There are many R129s on the market, but far fewer cars in really good condition. This guide will help you decide which SL is right for you, and find the best car to buy.

Thanks

I am immensely grateful to the many Mercedes-Benz specialists who shared their expertise with me: Brian Ellis from the UK Mercedes-Benz Club, Jonathan Aucott of Avantgarde Cars, Bruce Greetham at the SL Shop, Glenn Turnbull and Oliver Stone of Turnbull and Oliver, Richard Powell and Shaun Zealey. Mercedes-Benz itself also provided me with invaluable help; my thanks are due to Rory Lumsdon, Sophie Thompson and Olivia Frankel in the UK, and to Manuel Müller and Silvie Kiefer in Stuttgart.

Last but not least, it is a pleasure to thank once again the great team at Veloce Publishing, and in particular Rod Grainger, Lizzie Bennett and Sam Childs.

The author's late-model SL500.

Contents

The Essential Buyer's Guide™ currency
At the time of publication a BG unit of currency "●" equals approximately
£1.00/US$1.31/Euro€1.18. Please adjust to suit current exchange rates
using Sterling as the base currency.

1 Is it the right car for you?
– marriage guidance

Tall and short drivers

Most drivers should be comfortable, although those over 190cm (6ft 3in) may find space a little tight. The top mounting for the seatbelt moves automatically as you adjust the head restraint.

Weight of controls

The R129 is easy to handle, with automatic transmission on nearly all cars, and power steering. The accelerator requires a firm push, but you soon get used to it.

Will it fit the garage?

Length:	176in	4470mm
Width:	71in	1812mm
Height (with hardtop):	51in	1312mm

Interior space

Access to the front is good, but the rear seats are very cramped and best used for extra luggage. They are only fitted with lap belts, which may present problems if you wish to fit child seats. Cars sold in Australia, Japan and New Zealand, or fitted with the optional Bose sound system, did away with the rear seats altogether. Storage space inside is otherwise limited.

Luggage capacity

The boot (trunk) is of moderate capacity (265 litres/9.35ft³), but is regular in shape and claimed to take two golf bags. Removing the wind stop frees up more space.

Running costs

Any R129 is a heavy, relatively powerful car, and you inevitably pay the price at the pumps. Expect to see 20mpg (Imp)/17mpg (US) on the road from a 500SL, less

Comfortable front seats, but space in the back is limited. (Courtesy Mercedes-Benz Classic)

from the heavier 600SL. Later 24-valve V8s and the SL320 V6 are a bit more economical, the latter achieving up to 27mpg (Imp)/23mpg (US) when cruising.

Usability

The R129 can be used all year, thanks to its standard hardtop. Comprehensive safety equipment on cars built after 1995 includes side airbags and ESP.

Parts availability

Most mechanical parts and body panels are available. However, some electrical items, including certain relays and electronic control units (ECUs), as well as trim parts like the carpeted sill panels, are now harder

Soft top or hardtop? (Courtesy Mercedes-Benz Classic)

to find. In some cases, independent specialists produce good quality replacements.

Parts cost
Routine service items are surprisingly affordable, but major components and trim parts can be very dear. Tyres are increasingly expensive on newer and more powerful models with bigger wheels. In general, the V12-engined cars will be significantly more expensive to maintain.

Insurance
Costs should be reasonable, if you have another car as your daily driver and can insure the SL as a classic. Newer cars, or those used as sole or everyday cars, can be significantly more expensive to insure.

Investment potential
The R129 has already reached the bottom of the depreciation chart, and prices for good cars with low mileage and a full history have been going up for some time. In the longer term, the best investments will be special edition cars, such as the Mille Miglia, Silver Arrows or SL Editions, Designo and AMG models. Late-model SL600s, with the panoramic roof, should also fare well.

Foibles
The R129 has few quirks. The foot-operated parking brake may take some getting used to, especially for European drivers.

Plus points
Classy, elegant styling. Effortless performance (especially V8/V12 cars). Build quality and finish. High level of equipment (especially late models).

Rare and desirable SL55 AMG with panoramic roof. (Courtesy Mercedes-Benz Classic)

Minus points
Not an out-and-out sports car. Lack of rear seat room. Maintenance can be costly. Fuel consumption (in cities and when driven hard).

Alternatives
BMW 8-Series, Cadillac Allante, Jaguar XJS, Jaguar XK8/XKR, Porsche 928.

2 Cost considerations
– affordable, or a money pit?

Purchase price

You can find cars as cheap as ●x5000, but their previous owners may have skimped on servicing. Excellent examples from specialist dealers typically sell for ●x12,000-25,000, with the 500SL/SL500 worth a bit more than the six-cylinder models. Exceptional cars and limited editions can command up to ●x35,000. As the R129 emerges as a modern classic, prices are moving up: don't wait too long!

Servicing

In 1997, Mercedes introduced its ASSYST system, with variable service intervals depending on how the car is used. Earlier cars require an oil service at 9000 miles or 15,000km and an inspection service at 18,000 miles or 30,000km. The services at 36,000-mile/60,000km intervals are the major ones, so make sure that these have been carried out. High mileage isn't an issue, if the car has been regularly maintained.

For cars covering a low mileage, it is just as important to check that the car has been serviced regularly, ideally every year.
Brake fluid: change every two years.
Coolant: change every three years.
Sparkplugs: change every four years.

Parts prices

Prices shown are for parts supplied by Mercedes or reputable independent specialists and are for the first-generation 500SL/SL500 built from 1989-95, unless noted otherwise.

M119 V8 engine as fitted to 500SL. (Courtesy Mercedes-Benz Classic)

Mechanical parts

Air filter x20
Fuel filter x20
Oil filter x20
Battery x170
Catalytic converter x320
Exhaust (full system, non-catalyst) x2560
Brake discs/rotors (pair; front) x190
Brake pads (set; front) x80
Brake discs/rotors (pair; rear) x120
Brake pads (set; rear) x50
Engine wiring harness (refitted; SL320) x2160
Accessory drivebelt x20
Water pump (SL320) x120
Radiator (SL320) x460
Throttle body (refurbished) x870
Head gasket (300SL-24) x30
Camshaft oilers (set of 16) x310
Differential oil seal x10
Front anti-roll bar bush (each) x10
Front suspension: lower control bush kit x70
Front suspension top mount x60
Rear subframe bush kit x60
Rear spring x140
Shock absorber (front) x190
Shock absorber (rear) x200
ADS accumulator sphere (SL500 1998-2001) x260
Steering damper x40
Tyre (225/55 R16 Pirelli P7 Cinturato) x190

Body parts

Central locking vacuum pump (refurbished) x460
Roof control module (ECU) x1690
Soft top: complete x1140
Windstop (black) x130
Bonnet x1090
Under-bonnet insulation x60
Front wing x540
Front bumper assembly x1680
Rear bumper assembly x2080
Door x1690
Windscreen x420
Headlamp lens (halogen) x140
Tail light assembly x370
Carpet set x1330

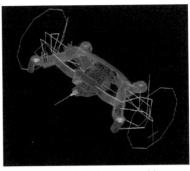
Rear suspension assembly.
(Courtesy Mercedes-Benz Classic)

Original design of alloy wheel, no longer available from Mercedes.
(Courtesy Mercedes-Benz Classic)

Wooden centre console is no longer available from Mercedes-Benz and may be expensive to find elsewhere.
(Courtesy Mercedes-Benz Classic)

Good points

The R129-series SL is a Grand Tourer *par excellence*, as well suited to sweeping across whole countries or states, as it is to cruising gently with the top down along

a sunny seaside road. Its engines – especially the V8 and V12 units – are powerful yet refined, and are ideally matched to Mercedes' smooth-shifting automatic transmissions. The ride is comfortable and handling reassuring. The R129 feels far more modern to drive than its predecessor, the R107. The high levels of safety equipment, especially on later models, should reassure partners who are worried about travelling in an older car.

Three cars in one: hardtop, soft top and fully open.
(Courtesy Mercedes-Benz Classic)

The R129 retains a timeless elegance and simply oozes sophistication and refinement. With its cosy hardtop for winter and electrically operated soft top in summer, the R129 is a car that can realistically be used every day all year round. Most cars are very well equipped, especially the final models built from 1998-2001. Indeed, the only major items of equipment missing, when compared with new cars on sale today, are parking sensors, and the latest navigation and in-car entertainment systems.

For would-be buyers who may be worried about maintaining a potentially unreliable older classic, the R129 can be a wonderful introduction to luxurious, top-down motoring. The cars are generally reliable and suffer relatively little from corrosion. With all of them now over 20 years old, however, they are increasingly accepted at club events and other meetings of classic cars.

Bad points

Ironically, it is the R129's modernity which may put off some potential purchasers. Its body wears protective plastic panels, rather than the chrome trim of Mercedes-Benz' older models, and it still feels quite contemporary to drive. The driving

experience may be too sanitised for some enthusiasts, and lacking in raw excitement. The V8 and V12 cars are certainly quick, the AMG models even more so, but the SL is too heavy and refined to be an out-and-out sports car. Only a tiny number of six-cylinder SLs were produced with a manual

Elegance personified: late-model SL500 with panoramic roof.
(Courtesy Mercedes-Benz Classic)

gear change, and this was notchy and made the foot-operated parking brake awkward to use.

The R129 is really only practical as a two-seater, and there was no direct equivalent to the SLC model in the 107 series. If you are looking for an open four-seater from the same era, you will have to to turn to the A124 cabrio, available with four or six-cylinder engines.

Magnificently impractical cream interior.

The hardtop insulates passengers from the elements as well as any fixed-head coupé, but is heavy (34kg/75lb) and cumbersome to remove, even for two people. Most owners will only remove and re-fit it once a year, and you will need a stand or extra space to store it.

All R129s should impress with their finish and build quality, and the earlier models used especially durable materials. The fine Nappa leather found on later cars, however, is more vulnerable to damage. Cars with light interior trim colours (mushroom, light grey and, especially, cream) show the marks and can wear badly. The author's car looked superb, but was hopelessly impractical, with leather, carpets and even overmats all in light cream!

Summary

For many would-be buyers, the R129 is now the most affordable – if not the only – way to enter the privileged circle of Mercedes SL ownership, with prices a fraction of the cars' cost when new. Values of the earlier R107 have soared out of reach for many first-time SL buyers. Meanwhile, some current R107 owners are now keeping them for special occasions, and are turning to the R129 as a second SL to drive more regularly. If you take this generation of SL for what it is – a superb two-seat GT – it is a part the R129 can play to perfection. Buy well and look after your car, and your investment will be amply repaid.

Cruising through the countryside with the top down.
(Courtesy Mercedes-Benz Classic)

4 Relative values
– which model for you?

The earliest R129-series SLs are now more than 30 years old, so, increasingly, it makes sense to buy on condition and mileage, rather than exact specification. All the cars came, as standard, with a hardtop and soft top, and nearly all were fitted with automatic transmission. During its 12-year life, the R129 was fitted with engines ranging from a 2.8-litre 'six' all the way to a 7.3-litre V12. Your choices will therefore come down to the generation of car and engine you prefer.

Which generation?

Built from 1989–2001, the R129 underwent two major face-lifts, in 1995 and 1998.

Cars from the original phase of production – from their introduction in 1989 until 1995 – can be recognised by their contrasting plastic side panels, three-part side grilles and traditional (non-digital) odometer. At launch, customers could choose from the six-cylinder 300SL and 300SL-24 and the V8-powered 500SL; the V12-engined 600SL followed in 1992. In 1993, the model designation was changed from, eg, 500SL to SL500, while new straight-six engines with four valves per cylinder in the SL280 and SL320 replaced the 300SL and 300SL-24.

Three-part side grille on first-generation model. (Courtesy Mercedes-Benz Classic)

In September 1995, Mercedes modernised the cars' appearance and updated their technical specifications. Second-generation cars can be identified by their body-coloured side panels with two-part side grilles, clear front indicator lenses and new alloy wheels. Inside, there was a new steering wheel and the odometer was now digital. Mechanically, a new five-speed automatic transmission replaced the four-speeder on the SL500 and SL600.

Standard-fit 'Monkar' 16in wheel on second-generation car.

New features available included ESP, BAS (Brake Assist), xenon (HID) headlamps and a panoramic roof.

By July 1998, the R129 was beginning to date, and Mercedes refreshed its appearance one last time. The final-generation cars had softer, more rounded lines, with new designs for door mirror, side indicator repeater and tail lights, as well as bold new alloy wheels. Inside, Mercedes improved the cars' equipment and trim, with sumptuous Nappa leather seats and chrome instrument rings. The biggest changes, however,

Nappa leather seats on final-generation car. (Courtesy Mercedes-Benz Classic)

were under the bonnet (hood), with new V6 units in the SL280 and SL320. In the SL500 a new V8, with three valves per cylinder, produced slightly less power than before, but – like all the new engines – boasted better fuel economy.

Which generation you choose will likely be a matter of model availability and your budget, with the final-generation cars (from 1998-2001) commanding the highest prices. Some observers consider the earlier cars to be better assembled, but, in truth, any R129 will seem superbly built in comparison to other makes or its own successor, the R230. In some areas, earlier cars used more durable materials (for the seat upholstery and door cards, for example); later cars, on the other hand, were better equipped, and more luxuriously appointed.

Watch out for cars which have been retro-fitted with lights or exterior trim from a newer model, or which stood unsold at dealerships when new. In case of doubt, take extra care when checking the paperwork.

Which engine?

Six, eight or twelve cylinders? The R129 offered an unprecedented range of engines, and not a diesel in sight!

The six-cylinder cars tend to be a little cheaper to buy and to maintain; the cars' weight takes the edge off their performance, but they are still refined cruisers. Mercedes-Benz' straight-six engines are renowned for their smoothness, while the 300SL-24 has a more sporting edge. The SL320 V6 is an excellent all-rounder. Only the six-cylinder cars were ever offered with a manual gearbox, but numbers sold outside Germany were tiny; most drivers will find the automatic ideally suited to the car.

M119 V8 engine, from a first-generation 500SL. (Courtesy Mercedes-Benz Classic)

For many R129 owners, the V8-engined 500SL/SL500 is the pick of the range, offering effortless performance without the front-end heaviness of the 600. Fuel consumption is a little higher than for the six-cylinder cars, but most owners cover modest annual mileages.

The V12-engined 600SL/SL600 is exceptionally smooth and faster still than the 500, but is very complex indeed. When the V8 is this good, do you really need the extra power?

The AMG cars are much more sporting in character, with more power and stiffer suspension. Of these, the SL60, sold from 1993-98, is – relatively speaking – the most common. The

V12 fills the engine bay of this early 600SL.

The ultimate SL.
(Courtesy Mercedes-Benz Classic)

SL55 AMG and ballistic SL73 AMG (whose V12 engine was used in the Pagani Zonda) were sold in tiny numbers from 1999–2001.

Special editions
In its final years of production, Mercedes produced countless special editions to sustain interest in the SL. Most commonly based on the SL500, these featured individual paint finishes and interior trim, often with two-tone leather and fine woods or aluminium on the centre console. These limited-run series – including the Mille Miglia, Silver Arrows, SL Edition, Final Edition and *designo* models – reach premium prices among collectors.

Distinctive interior trim on SL Edition. (Courtesy Mercedes-Benz Classic)

5 Before you view

– be well informed

To avoid a wasted journey, and the disappointment of finding that the car does not match your expectations, it will help if you're very clear about what questions you want to ask before you pick up the telephone. Some of these points might appear basic, but when you're excited about the prospect of buying your dream classic, it's amazing how some of the most obvious things slip the mind … You can also check the current values of the model which attracts you, in classic car magazines, which give both a price guide and auction results.

Where is the car?

Is it going to be worth travelling to the next county/state, or even across a border? A locally advertised car, although it may not sound very interesting, can add to your knowledge for very little effort, so make a visit – it might even be in better condition than expected.

Dealer or private sale

Establish early on if the car is being sold by its owner or by a trader. A private owner should have all the history, so don't be afraid to ask detailed questions. A dealer may have more limited knowledge of a car's history, but should have some documentation. A dealer may offer a warranty/guarantee (ask for a printed copy) and finance.

Cost of collection and delivery

A dealer may well be used to quoting for delivery by car transporter. A private owner may agree to meet you halfway, but only agree to this after you have seen the car at the vendor's address to validate the documents. Conversely, you could meet halfway and agree the sale, but insist on meeting at the vendor's address for the handover.

View – when and where

It is always preferable to view at the vendor's home or business premises. In the case of a private sale, the car's documentation should tally with the vendor's name and address. Arrange to view only in daylight and avoid a wet day. Most cars look better in poor light or when wet.

Reason for sale

Do make it one of the first questions. Why is the car being sold, and how long has it been with the current owner? How many previous owners?

Imports from Germany

There is often a wider range of SLs on sale in Germany. Some German-market cars, especially from the first generation of R129s, are less well equipped than in other markets, with cloth interiors and manual air-conditioning rather than climate control. Some home-market cars also came without the rear seats or (from 1991-93) a hardtop.

When you buy a car from another country, you may need to make changes to the number (license) plates, lighting (headlamps and indicators) and radio equipment. If you re-register a car from Germany or another EU country within the EU, you will need to obtain a European Certificate of Conformity (CoC) or – for cars first registered before 1996 – an attestation from the manufacturer.

Condition (body/chassis/interior/mechanicals)

Query the car's condition in as specific terms as possible – preferably citing the checklist items described in Chapter 9.

All original specification

An original equipment car is invariably of higher value than a customised version.

Matching data/legal ownership

• Do VIN/chassis, engine numbers and licence plate match the official registration document? Is the owner's name and address recorded in the official registration documents?

• For those countries that require an annual test of roadworthiness, does the car have a document showing it complies (an MOT certificate in the UK, which can be verified by the DVSA on 0300 123 9000 or online at gov.uk/check-mot-status)?

• If a smog/emissions certificate is mandatory, does the car have one?

• If required, does the car carry a current road fund license/licence plate tag?

• Does the vendor own the car outright? Money might be owed to a finance company or bank: the car could even be stolen. Several organisations will supply the data on ownership, based on the car's licence plate number, for a fee. Such companies can often also tell you whether the car has been 'written-off' by an insurance company. In the UK, these organisations can supply vehicle data:

HPI – 0113 222 2010
AA – 0800 316 3564
DVLA – 0300 790 6802
RAC – 0808 164 1923
Other countries will have similar organisations.

Insurance

Check with your existing insurer before setting out; your current policy might not cover you to drive the car if you do purchase it.

How you can pay

A cheque/check will take several days to clear and the seller may prefer to sell to a cash buyer. However, a banker's draft (a cheque issued by a bank) is as good as cash, but safer, so contact your own bank and become familiar with the formalities that are necessary to obtain one.

Certificate of Conformity essential to re-register car within Europe.

Buying at auction?

If the intention is to buy at auction, see Chapter 10 for further advice.

Professional vehicle check (mechanical examination)

There are often marque/model specialists who will undertake professional examination of a vehicle on your behalf. Owners clubs will be able to put you in touch with such specialists.

Other organisations that will carry out a general professional check in the UK are:

AA – 0800 056 8040 / www.theaa.com/vehicle-inspection (motoring organisation with vehicle inspectors)

RAC – 0330 159 0720 / www.rac.co.uk/buying-a-car/vehicle-inspections (motoring organisation with vehicle inspectors)

Other countries will have similar organisations.

Few official Mercedes dealers still sell R129s today.

6 Inspection equipment

– these items will really help

This book

This book is designed to be your guide at every step, so take it along, and use the check boxes to help you assess each area of the car you're interested in. Don't be afraid to let the seller see you using it.

Reading glasses (if you need them for close work)

Take your reading glasses, if you need them, to read documents and make close-up inspections.

Torch

A torch with fresh batteries will be useful for peering into the wheelarches and under the car.

Magnet (not powerful, a fridge magnet is ideal)

A magnet will help you check if the car is full of filler. Use the magnet to sample bodywork areas all around the car, but be careful not to damage the paintwork. Expect to find a little filler here and there, but not whole panels.

Probe (a small screwdriver works very well)

A small screwdriver can be used – with care – as a probe, particularly in the wheelarches and on the underside. With this, you should be able to check an area of severe corrosion, but be careful – if it's really bad, the screwdriver might go right through the metal!

Overalls

Be prepared to get dirty. Take along a pair of overalls, if you have them.

Mirror on a stick

Fixing a mirror at an angle on the end of a stick may seem odd, but you'll probably need it to check the condition of the underside of the car. It will also help you to peer into some of the important crevices. You can also use it, together with the torch, along the underside of the sills and on the floor.

Digital camera (or smartphone)

If you have a digital camera or smartphone, take it along so that, later, you can study some areas of the car more

Ask the seller to raise the bonnet to the service position for a better view.

closely. Take a picture of any part of the car that causes you concern, and seek a friend's opinion. Like the mirror on a stick, a 'selfie stick' may help you get your smartphone under the car.

A friend; preferably a knowledgeable enthusiast
Ideally, have a friend or knowledgeable enthusiast accompany you: a second opinion is always valuable.

Try and look underneath the car if you can.
(Courtesy Turnbull & Oliver)

MERCEDES-BENZ

Is it still as it left the showroom? (Courtesy Mercedes-Benz Classic)

Exterior

First impressions can tell you a lot about a secondhand car. A few minutes can often be enough to decide whether you should stay or walk away. Look at the exterior first. A few small scratches are inevitable, especially for cars which have been used regularly in cities. But dented panels, parking scrapes, scuffed alloy wheels and badly worn tyres all suggest a car which has been poorly cared for.

Look carefully along the line of the car on each side for dents or uneven panels, then step back from it to check for mismatched paint on different panels, which may be the result of poor accident repairs. Make sure that both doors, bonnet (hood) and boot (trunk) open without difficulty, using the standard vacuum-operated central locking. Check that the hardtop and soft top – both of which came as standard on all but a handful of R129s – are with the car. If the soft top is in place when you arrive, it should appear taut and clean; look carefully for any tears in the fabric or seams, or cracks and discolouration in the plastic window panels. Raising or lowering the soft top takes only 30 seconds, so why not test it straightaway? If the hardtop is fitted, continue with the rest of your checks, but ask the seller to remove it if you decide the car deserves a more detailed examination.

A bump in a car park or narrow lane can dislodge the mirror glass.

The onset of corrosion lets down this split-rim alloy.

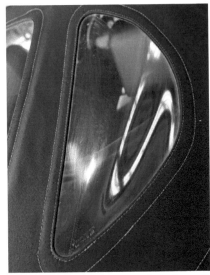

Make sure the window panels in the soft top are clear and free from cracks.

Interior and boot (trunk)

The interior of the R129 is beautifully appointed; the first- and second-generation models are particularly durable and should stand up well to many years of use. This can sometimes tempt unscrupulous sellers to wind back the clock. Does the overall condition of the car match the mileage shown on the odometer? Heavy wear on the pedals, steering wheel rim or driver's seat side bolster are all indicative of high mileage. Cars with light-coloured interiors are harder to keep in tiptop condition.

Look for excessive wear on the steering wheel rim.

Look for signs of water leaks in the footwells and in the boot. These can be the result of perished seals, leaks from the soft top or a rusted plenum chamber. If any non-standard equipment – such as a mobile phone – has been fitted, are there any screw holes or other unsightly marks left behind?

Checking all the electrical equipment on an R129 takes some time (see Chapter 9 for more details), but if you notice anything wrong during your initial inspection of the car, start to worry!

Removing non-standard equipment like this phone holder can leave ugly marks.

Not a good start! The grille on this SL will need to be replaced.

Well-travelled 600SL.

The engine compartment

Pop open the bonnet and take a quick look at the engine: it needn't be immaculately clean, but should be free from obvious leaks, damaged hoses and trailing wires. If the car has been standing, look underneath for signs of oil or other fluid leaks.

Which model is it?

Before asking the seller for a test drive, there are a few more things you can check quickly and easily. Obvious though it sounds, the first thing to confirm is exactly which model you are looking at. Is the car you are viewing as described? Many SLs were 'de-badged,' with the model designation removed when they were first delivered. The differences in appearance between each generation of R129 (described in Chapter 4) are quite subtle, especially when you first start looking at cars on sale, but

AMG badge ... but not an AMG car!

can hide important changes in the cars' mechanical specifications. The VIN number (see below) will help you establish exactly which year and model of SL you are looking at. If you are tempted by an AMG model, is it genuine? Mercedes built fewer than 1000 R129-based AMGs; authentic cars are especially rare in right-hand drive. Be wary of standard cars which may just have a badge or minor trim parts added.

Modifications

As the R129 moves towards classic status, the market is placing an increasing premium on originality. You may see upgraded stereos or non-standard alloy wheels on some cars, but more substantial modifications should be avoided. They will make the car harder to sell and are more likely to reduce, rather than increase, its value. In the longer term, cars which are completely original will command the best prices. You may even come across a dedicated enthusiast who has kept the original brochures.

Scissor doors and massive wheels will put off many buyers.

Even aftermarket stereo speakers can detract from a car's value.

Period brochures: often a sign of a dedicated collector.

Is it genuine and legal?

However attractive the car may look at first, it's essential that the paperwork is in order. First of all, does the VIN (the 17-digit Vehicle Identification Number) on the car tally with that on the registration/title document? On the R129, you can find this pressed into the metal at the rear of the engine compartment close to the right-hand suspension top mount, and also on a sticker in the driver's door jamb. Make sure that the VIN hasn't been tampered with, and take a note or photograph of it for reference. You can look it up online later to confirm the year of manufacture of the car or check its service history in the Mercedes-Benz dealer network. European and North American VIN numbers are formatted differently, but each will help you confirm the specification of the car. The key part of the VIN to pick out is for the model: in the examples below, this is highlighted in red.

Europe: WDB129**0682**F123456
North America: WDBFA**68**F61F123456

058: SL280	059: SL280 (V6)	060: 300SL
061: 300SL-24	063: SL320	064: SL320 (V6)
066: 500SL	067: 500SL/SL500/SL60 AMG	068: SL500/SL55 AMG
076: 600SL/SL600/SL73 AMG		

Independent organisations (see Chapter 5) will also let you check that there is no finance outstanding on the car, and no record of serious accident damage. If something doesn't seem right here, walk away now. At best, you may have problems registering the car; at worst, it may be stolen or unroadworthy. Does the seller's name and address appear on the registration or title document? How many owners has the car had? Frequent changes of ownership, especially recently, may mean their owners haven't been able to keep on top of repairs, potentially leaving you with the bill to put things right. If you are buying privately, be sure to view the car at the owner's home address, so that you can check this tallies with the paperwork for the car.

If all these details are correct, ask to see evidence of the car's service history including, if possible, invoices for work done, showing the parts which have been replaced. If the car requires an annual roadworthiness certificate in your country (such as the MoT test in the UK), make sure that this is current, and note any advisories, indicating work that should be done. You may be able to use these to negotiate a reduction in the price you pay. Finally, make sure that the mileage on the car's odometer matches that on the service documentation or test certificates.

Road test

If this is your first drive in an SL, it should be a moment to savour. Before setting out, make sure that the insurance covers you to drive, and check that the indicators, lights and wipers all work. Try and start the car from cold if possible: the engine should start easily and idle smoothly. Look in the rear-view mirror (or have a friend stand behind the car) for any signs of smoke from the exhaust when starting or accelerating. For first- and second-generation cars fitted with an oil pressure gauge, this should move up to the maximum reading (of 3 bar) as soon as you give the engine some revs.

Keep the radio off (you can test that when the car is parked up later) and lower the roof (or at least the driver's window), so that you can hear any rattles or untoward noises from the engine, suspension or exhaust system. Let the engine come up to temperature before revving it hard. Try and drive the car on a variety of roads, including some out-of-town stretches where you can open up the engine, and also test the cruise control (if fitted). Whether in-line six, V6, V8 or V12, all the engines fitted to the R129-series should be delightfully smooth throughout the rev range. Keep an eye on the water temperature, which should remain steady, even in city traffic. If the car does show any signs of overheating, the water pump or viscous coupling for the fan may be faulty.

On cars fitted with automatic transmission (the vast majority), check the transmission operates correctly in the different modes (including the Economy and Winter settings, where provided) and when selecting the gears manually. The rare manual transmission cars have a stiff and notchy change. If the clutch is slipping or has a high biting point, it's probably on its way out, so you will need to budget for a replacement.

Try and find a clear stretch of open road, where you can take your hands off the wheel: the car should continue to run straight. If it doesn't, closer examination and an alignment check will be required. A small amount of free play around the straight-ahead position is typical of the recirculating ball system fitted to the R129, but it should not be excessive.

Apply the brakes a few times: they should operate smoothly. Any judder usually means that the discs (rotors) are warped or corroded and will need to be replaced. When there is nobody behind you – and after warning the seller first! – try making an emergency stop: the car should pull up straight, without veering to either side. With sufficient pressure, and particularly if the road is wet or greasy, you should feel the standard anti-lock brakes (ABS) kick in as the brake pedal pulses under your foot. Any failings here will need further investigation.

Make sure too that the parking brake can be applied and released smoothly, with an audible click, and that it will hold the car securely. On cars with automatic transmission, many owners simply put the transmission in Park. Lack of use can cause the parking brake to seize up and the car to fail an MoT test or similar roadworthiness inspection.

When you return to the seller's premises or home, take a final look under the bonnet, and on the ground, for any fresh oil or coolant leaks.

Only buy a car from an individual who can prove that they are the person named in the car's registration document (V5C in the UK) and, preferably, at the address shown in the document. Also check that the VIN or chassis number/frame and engine numbers of the car match the numbers in the registration document.

Make the most of the test drive to check the car performs well. (Courtesy Mercedes-Benz Classic)

8 Key points

– where to look for problems

Beautifully built and effortlessly refined, the R129-series SL should be as enjoyable to drive today as it was when new; but its solid feel and generous equipment come at a price, adding weight to the car and complexity to its systems.

Living the dream: open-top SL beside the sea. (Courtesy Mercedes-Benz Classic)

Engine and mechanicals

The engines which Mercedes used in the SL range are fundamentally strong, well-engineered units, and with regular maintenance, they are capable of high mileages. So, too, most of the automatic transmissions fitted to nearly all the cars sold. The only exceptions are the earlier type of five-speed automatic transmission (722.5) fitted to the six-cylinder cars and, above all, the redoubtable V12-engined 600SL/SL600. Writing for the Mercedes-Benz Club in North America, Bud Cloninger described this as "a car that only a mother could love."

The cars' weight, allied to their strong performance, takes its toll on brakes and suspension components alike. With the exception of the optional Adaptive Damping System (ADS), however, maintenance of these parts is straightforward, and parts prices are generally reasonable.

Electrics

It is the cars' ancillary systems which need to be checked most carefully when buying an R129 today: the SL has a bewildering array of hydraulic components, electric motors and electronic control units (ECUs), controlling everything from the pop-up roll-over bar to the position of the head restraints, from the soft top mechanism

An outstanding and durable engine, the M119 V8 from the 500SL. (Courtesy Mercedes-Benz Classic)

25

Cutaway model shows just how complex the R129 really is.

to the lockable centre cubby. As new features such as Brake Assist System (BAS) and satellite navigation were added, the cars became ever more complex. It is essential to check that everything still works as intended, as problems with these systems can be difficult and expensive to put right.

Bodywork and interior
The R129 has a good reputation for rust, with fewer problems than its predecessor, the R107. Inside too, the car is superbly finished, especially the first- and second-generation cars; the final cars traded some durability for even more luxury and equipment.

So much of the pleasure of owning a R129 comes from its year-round appeal: a comfortable closed coupé in winter and an open-air tourer in summer. To ensure those pleasures continue trouble-free, checking the condition and smooth operation of the hardtop and soft top is vital, and the cost of repairs should not be underestimated.

Hardtop or soft top? No need to choose! (Courtesy Mercedes-Benz Classic)

9 Serious evaluation

– 60 minutes for years of enjoyment

Score each section using the boxes as follows:
4 = excellent; 3 = good; 2 = average; 1 = poor. The totting-up procedure is detailed at the end of the chapter. Be realistic in your marking!

If you've come this far, well done! The paperwork is in order and the car looks promising. Now is the time to take a really thorough look over it, bearing in mind the points already mentioned in the last two chapters. Try and work your way systematically round the car, so that you don't miss any nagging details. Start outside with a close look at the bodywork, before turning your attention to the interior, and, finally, the engine and underbody.

Exterior

First impressions

Make sure that you can view the car outdoors and in daylight, preferably in good weather. The car should be clean; it's hard to judge the condition of paint under a layer of dirt. Begin by stepping back from the car and noting how it sits on the road. You should be able to fit two fingers between the top of the tyre and the wheelarch. Does the car appear to sag on either side or at one end? That could be the result of a problem with the suspension, particularly if the car is fitted with the sophisticated Adaptive Damping System (ADS).

Some owners may have lowered the suspension: do the wheels still clear the wheelarches, especially at full lock? Will the front spoiler grind on speed bumps? This is most likely to occur if the car has also been fitted with an aftermarket bodykit. Run your hand underneath the front spoiler to check for any cracks or damage to the paintwork. Later cars with ADS had a front-end lift feature, operated by a specific dashboard switch, which makes damage like this easier to avoid – as long as the system is still working!

Still showroom-fresh? First impressions count for a lot.

Bodywork

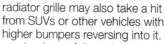

Look at the overall condition of the body: are the panels straight and crease-free, without any serious dents? Crouch down and look along the side of the car, to check if anything seems out of line. The panel gaps should be consistent right around the car.

The SL's bodywork is very susceptible to minor bumps and scratches in everyday use. Rear parking sensors were never fitted as standard, so the rear bumper (fender) is particularly vulnerable. If the front or rear bumper has been scraped, is the panel itself still solidly attached to the car and free from cracks? The

Panel gaps should be straight and even.

radiator grille may also take a hit from SUVs or other vehicles with higher bumpers reversing into it.

Look carefully at the plastic panels on each side of the car. If these are loose, water can get in, causing corrosion. This may also tell you that the car has been poorly repaired after an accident; so, too, can rear model badges applied in the wrong position on the boot (trunk) lid or different types of licence plate at each end of the car. Open both doors, bonnet (hood) and the boot fully: check for unpainted bolts and welding seams instead of the factory-applied spot welds. All of these may point to accident damage and will require further investigation.

Nothing serious: an unsightly dent next to the three-pointed star on this SL.

Paintwork

There are few, if any, paintwork problems unique to the R129. Whichever colour you choose, make sure that the paint appears even and consistent across all the panels. The nose section is most exposed to stone chips, so a repainted front spoiler may even be a sign of a meticulous owner who has taken good care of the car.

A difference in shade between adjacent steel panels may suggest that the car has been repainted after an accident. If you are unused to Mercedes' cars from the 1990s, you may at first think that the plastic side panels have been mismatched to the bodywork, but, in fact, Mercedes deliberately applied a two-tone finish, with separate paint codes. You will find more guidance on assessing paintwork condition in Chapter 14.

Different colour for the bumpers and side cladding on this early R129. (Courtesy Mercedes-Benz Classic)

Body corrosion

The R129-series SLs generally have a good reputation for their resistance to rust, but the first models are now over 30 years old, so careful examination is essential. Since the cars were such great all-round GTs, some owners will have used them throughout the year. As a result, they may have been more exposed to winter weather and roads treated with salt: pay particular attention to the condition of

Often a place where rust is found, this front wing is still in excellent condition.

the underbody and suspension components if you are buying a car in an area with harsh winters. Inspecting an R129 is helped by the fact that most corrosion will be readily visible; unlike its predecessor, the R107, whose engine bulkhead could rust away unnoticed.

Of the main body panels, the front wings are most liable to rust, especially where they meet the front bumper. This needn't be a deal-breaker though, as the wings bolt on and are not unduly expensive to replace. Rust around the jacking points is less of an issue than on the W124-series cars from the same period; unclipping the jacking point covers, however, is still a quick way of checking for corrosion along the sills. Do take special care though when looking at the wheelarches, and run your hand around the inside of them to feel for patches of rust. Some cars, notably in North America, may have been fitted with aftermarket chrome wheelarch trims, which can trap water and conceal rust.

Rust is already taking hold at the base of this radio aerial.

Other places to check for corrosion include the base of the radio aerial (antenna) – where bubbling paint will be a sure-fire giveaway, the corners of the A-pillars and the side indicator repeaters (when fitted). Underneath the car, the front suspension mounting points are particularly exposed, especially in areas with frequent cold and wet weather.

Wheels

All R129-series SLs were fitted as standard with alloy wheels, but the design and specifications of these evolved considerably during the cars' lifetime, with their diameter increasing from 16in to 18in. Mercedes progressively developed the cars' suspension to match the bigger wheels; beware of early cars with uprated wheels, as these upgrades can put extra stress on the suspension components or cause imbalance.

Complex split-rim 'Albireo' wheel, as fitted to the Silver Arrows special edition.

Like most alloys, the wheels on the R129 are vulnerable to kerbing damage, especially on cars used extensively in cities. The coating on some wheels can lift, starting from the edge, allowing corrosion to set in. You may also see the onset of corrosion in the form of blistering around the bolt holes.

Refurbishing alloy wheels is a service offered by many specialists. On the R129, the wheels fitted to later cars are the most complex (and therefore

expensive) to recondition. Some later types of wheel had a polished outer flange, whilst others – notably the 18in wheels fitted to AMG models and some limited-edition cars – were of split-rim construction, requiring them to be disassembled before they can be refurbished.

Corrosion is starting to bubble away on this alloy wheel.

Soft top: mechanism

4 3 2 1

We take electrically operated soft tops for granted today, but Mercedes' power-operated top created a sensation when the R129 was launched. Today, it is one of the most important parts of the car to check thoroughly. If the car you come to view has its hardtop in place, insist on having it removed; allow yourself plenty of time to check the soft top mechanism works perfectly and to examine the fabric and window panels. If the soft top fails to operate, be ready to walk away.

Even by today's standards, the soft top mechanism is fearsomely complex, with 15 pressure cylinders, 11 solenoid valves and 17 limit sequences to ensure it works quickly (the complete operation should take 30 seconds) and safely. Thankfully, the mechanisms themselves have a good reputation for reliability, as the parts and labour costs entailed are high. The high-pressure hydraulic system may, however, sometimes suffer leaks. These will show up as stains around the sunvisors or the hydraulic rams in the soft top stowage area. Take a careful look in the stowage area for signs of corrosion as well. In general, it is a good idea to raise and lower the roof regularly, so that the mechanism – and the top itself – stay in good condition. Evidence that the hydraulic fluid for the soft top mechanism (in a reservoir under the boot floor) has been changed is another positive indication of an owner who has taken good care of the car.

The folding soft top mechanism demonstrated on a cutaway car at the Retro Classics show in Stuttgart.

What can be more problematic, however, is the electronic control unit (ECU) which controls the mechanism for the soft top: this is located under the rear seat (or luggage shelf). If an attempt is made to start a car with a flat battery, the spike in voltage can 'fry' the ECU. The soft top may then fail to operate altogether, or become stuck halfway. If you suspect a faulty ECU, first try opening both windows, switching the engine on and off, and pressing the brake pedal as hard as you can: this has been known to 'trick' the ECU into re-setting itself.

The soft top is controlled by the large red switch on the centre console: if this flashes red, but does not function correctly, the problem may simply be that the micro-switch for the front latch needs adjustment.

If the soft top mechanism does fail altogether – or you have a flat battery and urgently need to raise the top – there is an emergency procedure, described in the owner's manual. For this you will need the emergency release tool: make sure it is still present in the standard toolkit.

Master switch to operate the folding soft top. (Courtesy Mercedes-Benz Classic)

Complete toolkit with the emergency soft top release tool in the middle.

Soft top: condition

The soft top itself is surprisingly simple in construction. Its lifetime has been estimated at 10-15 years, after which the material may wear or the waterproofing fail. You can check the latter by running a glass of water down the top: it should pearl off the fabric and not soak in. Frequent use of car washes will reduce life expectancy of the material.

All R129s had three-section plastic windows set into the soft top; glass windows were never offered. The panels should be clear and free from cracks. In practice, they tend to discolour or go milky over time. Even tiny cracks gradually spread, leading to the risk of water leaks and stains.

Complete replacement soft tops with the original OEM-specification 'Sonnenland' fabric are now hard to obtain; third-party alternatives are available,

The stitching and window panels on this soft top are still in excellent condition.

The windstop folded down behind the front seats.

but their quality can vary, with some materials causing greater wind noise at speed. It may be tempting to save money and replace only the window sections, but the seams can let in water.

The detachable windstop makes high-speed cruising with the hood down much more comfortable. It became standard in 1993 and a dedicated storage cover was provided for it inside the boot. Check that the car you are buying has it, or haggle on the price so that you can buy one later.

Hardtop [4] [3] [2] [1]

The R129 was the last Mercedes SL to be equipped with a detachable hardtop. The hardtop should be completely free from leaks and impressively quiet. It was fitted as standard to all cars sold outside Germany, so don't accept any excuses if it is missing. Replacing or retro-fitting a hardtop is an expensive undertaking, complicated by changes to the seal design in 1992 and differences between the all-metal and panoramic (glass) roofs.

Even though it is made of alloy, the hardtop is still heavy (34kg/75lb) and needs two people to remove it. The panoramic roof is heavier yet; it was available as an option on the SL600 from 1993 and on other models from 1995.

Be sure to take off the hardtop, and look for signs of rust around the bottom rear sides, especially with the panoramic roof. The connector cable for the heated rear windscreen must be unplugged manually; check for signs of damage if it has been forcibly removed, which may prevent it from working. With the hardtop off, look too at the condition of the seals, which can dry out over time. If the hardtop squeaks during your test drive, a little silicon grease applied to the seals can often help.

If you plan on using your SL with the hardtop removed much of the time, it's well worth investing in a tailor-made stand from a company such as Special Vehicle Services (www.specialvehicle.co.uk), as the hardtop can be damaged if stored incorrectly. Manual and electric hoists are also available to make removing the top an easy, one-person job.

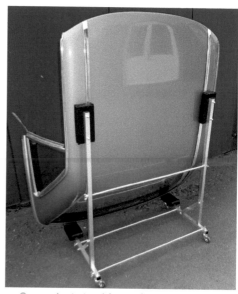

Convenient stand for an SL hardtop, here, showing an earlier R107 hardtop in position. (Courtesy SVS)

Glass [4] [3] [2] [1]

Examine the windscreen, side windows and rear screen in turn. If any of the windows have been tinted, is the depth of tint within the legally allowable limits in your country? Is the film used in good condition, or showing signs of cracks or lifting off?

The condition of the windscreen is especially important, as it is most likely to be damaged by stone chips. A crack in the driver's line of sight may cause the car to fail a roadworthiness inspection such as the MoT test in the UK. Earlier R129s have been known to suffer from a 'blooming' effect on the windscreen glass. At first merely unsightly, this can spread to the driver's field of view and may again be picked up during a safety inspection. A replacement windscreen is reasonably priced (by Mercedes-Benz standards, at least) and could be used as a bargaining point if the car looks good otherwise.

Interior

First impressions

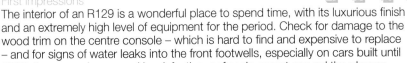

The interior of an R129 is a wonderful place to spend time, with its luxurious finish and an extremely high level of equipment for the period. Check for damage to the wood trim on the centre console – which is hard to find and expensive to replace – and for signs of water leaks into the front footwells, especially on cars built until 1992: these may be caused by defective roof seals or rust around the plenum chamber. Are the carpets still clean and in good condition? Replacement floor mats are no longer available from Mercedes, but high-quality alternatives (using the original patterns) are available from independent specialists such as Classic Mercedes Mats (www.classicmercedesmats.co.uk) in the UK.

Aftermarket mats help protect this cream interior.

Seats and upholstery

The front seats in the R129 are an engineering feat in their own right, and were awarded multiple prizes and some 20 patents. Their frames are made from lightweight but high-strength magnesium castings, and incorporate the seatbelt mountings. With motors to adjust their position in ten different ways (even the head restraint moves with the top mounting for the seatbelt), they are supremely

Assembly line shot shows the complex construction of the seat. (Courtesy Mercedes-Benz Classic)

comfortable, but also highly complex. Although not standard at first, many cars were fitted with a convenient memory function for the seats.

Should the seat motors break down, you will be looking at an expensive repair and – despite the provision of a mechanical back-up procedure – a potential fail during a statutory roadworthiness inspection. Fortunately, complete failures are rare, but it is a key point to check inside the car.

The leather upholstery fitted to the majority of cars should ideally be conditioned every six months, to keep it supple. This is especially important if the car has been used a lot with the hood down and exposed to sunlight, so take particular care with models on sale in US states like California or Florida, or which have been used as holiday cars in continental Europe. The Nappa leather used in the final generation of cars is wonderfully soft and luxurious, but less durable; it needs even more care to maintain its appearance, especially in light colours.

As with most cars, the side bolster on the driver's seat is most vulnerable to wear. Look too for signs of damage to the speaker grilles in the doors (which can be scuffed by shoes when getting in and out) and around the door handles.

Electric seat adjustment panel and still pristine speaker grille. (Courtesy Mercedes-Benz Classic)

This driver's seat bolster is beginning to wear.

Boot (trunk)

⁴ ³ ² ¹

If you see any signs of damp in the boot, check the condition of the seals, which may have perished with age and so allow water to get in. It's also worth examining the high-level rear brakelight, which can work loose. This will let water into the boot lid, and cause staining to the trim, or even corrosion on the emergency warning triangle (which should be clipped to the boot lid). Corrosion in the boot is otherwise rare, but take a look under the carpet and, especially, around the battery.

Luggage compartment, with stowage for windstop.

Rust along the bottom of this warning triangle is a sure sign that water has found its way in.

Electrics

This is without doubt the single most important area to check when considering an R129. Features such as the soft top mechanism, emergency roll-over bar and central locking (which extends to the storage compartments inside the car) combine electric and hydraulic systems. Even early R129s are extremely complicated, with electric adjustment for the steering wheel, head restraints and even the interior mirror!

Early cars had separate ECUs for each system, while later cars gained ever more equipment and moved on to integrated BUS circuitry. Like many

Be sure to check that the roll-over bar pops up using the switch. (Courtesy Mercedes-Benz Classic)

manufacturers, however, Mercedes was still learning its way around these new electronic systems, and faults which arise can prove difficult to diagnose and repair.

Instruments and controls

With the car parked outside and the engine running, take your time to check the operation of every single switch. If the seller objects, be ready to walk away. The instruments on the SL are clear and comprehensive, and all should be in working order. The mechanical odometer on first-generation cars can fail; if the car you are looking at has had a replacement unit fitted, take extra care when reviewing the other service documents available, which should corroborate the car's total mileage.

Again on early cars, if all the dashboard warning lights are on, this may be due to a faulty indicator relay. This isn't a big job to repair, but you

4 3 2 1

Allow plenty of time to check all of the controls. (Courtesy Mercedes-Benz Classic)

should insist that the seller gets it fixed and that it isn't hiding another, more serious, problem.

The R129 used Mercedes' distinctive single windscreen wiper, which 'jumps' up to clean the uppermost corners of the screen. If the weather is dry, be ready to throw a bucket of water over the screen so that you can test it properly. A slow or stiff mechanism may need nothing more than a squirt of WD40™ or similar lubricant, but if it has seized, replacing the motor is an expensive job.

1994 audio system: Mercedes-branded, but still with a cassette deck.

Audio systems

Most R129-series SLs will originally have been fitted with the best in-car entertainment systems available at the time. During the 12 years of the R129's lifecycle, however, these systems evolved enormously: from the original Becker-branded radio/cassette players of the first cars (which are sought-after classic accessories in their own right today) to multi-CD players, and even a primitive form of satellite navigation (all in a single-DIN dashboard unit) at the end of the car's production. Check that all the functions operate as they should, including the radio aerial, and that any security codes are still with the car.

It may be tempting to replace the original unit with a modern set offering MP3 playback, DAB or Sirius radio and Bluetooth connectivity, especially if you plan on using the car regularly. If you are buying the SL as a future collector's car, however, look for an original set (which specialists can restore to full working order).

Radio aerials can stick halfway, but are easily replaced.

Alarms

In the UK, insurers required that SLs were fitted with an aftermarket alarm – often a Scorpion unit installed by Mercedes-Benz dealers. These can play up, and, with parts no longer available, it is frequently easier to remove them altogether than try to repair them. Mercedes' own alarm, fitted to later cars, featured red and green warning lights in the interior mirror: this can be hard to repair without damaging the brittle plastic of the mirror housing. In any case, a fully functioning alarm is a bonus.

FITTED WITH A
**MERCEDES-BENZ (UK) LTD
APPROVED
ALARM SYSTEM**

Window sticker for UK dealer-fit alarm.

Lights

First-generation R129s were fitted with halogen headlamps, after which xenon (HID) headlamps became available. Although less powerful, halogen lamps are easier to find and cheaper to replace. Whichever type is fitted, check them – and the low-slung foglamps – for stone chips or other damage.

The indicators on early cars have been known to malfunction, so check these work on both sides at front and rear. For cars with clear indicator lenses at the front, make sure that these show a strong orange colour: the orange bulbs can fade over time,

Xenon headlamps and clear indicator lenses on this later car.

which can result in the car failing a roadworthiness inspection.

If the interior light fails to come on, it may be nothing more serious than a dirty contact on the door switch.

A/C sticker under the bonnet shows the refrigerant required.

Air-conditioning

Mercedes' air-conditioning system should deliver ice-cold air. If it doesn't, don't be fobbed off with stories that it only needs recharging. If the evaporator has failed, the entire dashboard will have to come out, a labour-intensive (and therefore costly) job.

Battery

With a big engine to turn over and so much electrical equipment on board, the R129 needs a powerful battery, which should be replaced regularly. The battery on the author's own car failed after only four years. Ask the seller when the battery was last changed and, if necessary, budget on getting a new one. A trickle charger is also a wise investment, to keep the battery in good condition.

Trim removed for easier access to the battery.

Engine and mechanicals
Under the bonnet (hood): first impressions

In common with many Mercedes-Benz models of the period, the bonnet can be lifted to a special service position at 90°, which gives great access to the engine. The soundproofing under the bonnet often

This latch opens the bonnet to the service position.

disintegrates due to the heat generated by the engine: it looks unsightly, but is easy to replace.

Take a look at the overall condition of the engine bay: are all the belts and hoses – including the polyrib accessory drivebelt – free from cracks or other damage? Can you see any rust, perhaps around the plenum chamber? If left untreated, water can end up leaking into the footwells. The chassis legs should appear straight: if they look out of alignment, that should alert you to the possibility of accident damage.

Check the accessory drivebelt for cracks.

This sound-deadening panel definitely needs replacing.

With the engine out, the chassis legs can be clearly seen.

General mechanical issues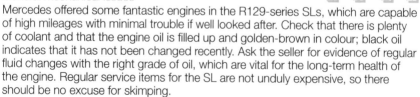

Mercedes offered some fantastic engines in the R129-series SLs, which are capable of high mileages with minimal trouble if well looked after. Check that there is plenty of coolant and that the engine oil is filled up and golden-brown in colour; black oil indicates that it has not been changed recently. Ask the seller for evidence of regular fluid changes with the right grade of oil, which are vital for the long-term health of the engine. Regular service items for the SL are not unduly expensive, so there should be no excuse for skimping.

The electronic systems on these engines are complex though, and can sometimes play up as the cars age. If the car you are viewing has any difficulty starting, or runs poorly, this could be due to problems with one of the ECUs, such as the spark controller ECU, which can be expensive to replace.

Scoring: score **one** of the following four sections (on the usual 4-3-2-1 scale), depending on which engine is fitted to the car you are assessing.

In-line six-cylinder engines: 300SL, 300SL-24 and SL280/320 4 3 2 1

Also used in the W124-series cars, these engines are renowned for their silken power delivery and longevity, with mileages in excess of 300,000 miles (500,000km) not uncommon.

Some engines, particularly those built between 1993 and 1995, have been known to suffer from problems with the wiring harness: the insulating material breaks down, which can cause misfires and uneven running, particularly if the damage extends back to the ECU. The looms are brittle and can be damaged during service work when the plugs or head gasket are changed. Replacement harnesses are no longer available from Mercedes, but can be tracked down through independents, or specially made up.

300SL-24 power plant. (Courtesy Mercedes-Benz Classic)

The 24-valve engine in the 300SL-24 is more sporting in nature. It is less prone to wiring harness issues, but – like all the 'straight-sixes' – can suffer from head gasket problems, particularly towards the back of the engine. Check for signs of oil and water mixing together to form a 'mayonnaise' under the coolant and oil filler caps, as this will cause serious damage to the engine.

V6 engines: SL280/320 4 3 2 1

The two V6 engines have developed a good reputation in service. One weak spot, however, is the crankshaft balancer, which can disintegrate, taking the timing case down with it. An updated replacement part overcomes this risk and is worth fitting on a preventative basis. A few issues have also been reported with the mass airflow (MAF) sensor, but replacements are available.

Immaculately presented 320 V6.

V8 engines: 500SL/SL500 and SL60 AMG 4 3 2 1

The M119 V8 fitted to first- and second-generation 500SL/SL500 models is widely considered one of Mercedes' best-ever power plants. Pre-1996 cars can suffer from moisture in the distributor cap, which will cause misfires and rough idling. A later design of cap can be fitted to overcome this.

Over time, the plastic camshaft oilers can degrade, causing a 'tappety' sound; these can be replaced, for about ●x310 for a set of 16. The plastic timing chain guides can also break down, causing the timing chain to

Four-valve M119 V8 on the 500SL at launch. (Courtesy Mercedes-Benz Classic)

jump, with the disastrous consequences that can be imagined! Evidence that these have been replaced is reassurance well worth having.

There are no additional points to watch for on the larger 6-litre unit fitted to the SL60 AMG.

The three-valve-per-cylinder engine fitted to the final-generation cars has proven largely unproblematic, but look for oil leaks from the front left-hand side of the engine, and from the rear main oil seal (between the engine and gearbox), which may show up under the car.

V12 engines: 600SL/SL600

When the cars were new, the V12 reputedly had the lowest warranty claims of

Nec plus ultra: the 7.3-litre AMG V12 engine. (Courtesy Mercedes-Benz Classic)

any Mercedes engine. As the years have gone by, however, its unrivalled complexity makes it a daunting prospect. Many dealers will now steer clear of any but the very best, low-mileage SL600s from the end of production.

The wiring harness problems which affect some of the 'straight-sixes' afflict the V12 too ... with the added complication that there are two looms, one for each bank of the engine. This engine also suffers from oil leaks from the front cover, which can ruin the alternator and any coolant or air hoses nearby. Space around the huge engine is very tight, resulting in high under-bonnet operating temperatures, and leaving precious little room for maintenance work.

Exhaust system

The exhaust system on the R129 is generally long-lived, but the rubber mountings can perish and the bolts corrode, allowing the pipes to work loose and rattle.

Poor quality fuel, or knocks from below, can cause the low-mounted catalytic converter to fail. Give it a thump with your hand and listen out. If you hear a clatter from the exhaust, check first that the shield has not worked loose, which is a quick and inexpensive repair. If not, that may mean that the catalytic converter has had it ... and an expensive bill to replace it. If a seller owns up to problems with the 'cat' and says he has simply removed it, move on:

Check all the exhaust mountings. (Courtesy Turnbull & Oliver)

the car's lambda sensor will be affected and the car will likely fail a statutory smog/emissions test.

Transmission

Mercedes has long enjoyed a tremendous reputation for the quality of its automatic transmissions, and those fitted to the R129 are no exception. Clonking or high-pitched whining noises, particularly on high-mileage cars, could mean problems with the differential; check for oil leaks from the diff too, as overhauls are expensive. If you can look at the car on a lift, test for movement on the propshaft, which may indicate that the gear selector rod bushes are worn. Corrosion on the transmission cooler pipes may result in leaks and the eventual loss of all fluid from the system.

The older four-speed 'box is very tough and should shift smoothly, albeit quite slowly, and kickdown needs a real push. The original five-speed automatic (722.5) offered on the six-cylinder cars is more complex and less reliable at higher mileages (typically after 100,000 miles/160,000km), with the risk of slipping in reverse or an inoperative fifth gear.

The electronically controlled 5G-Tronic transmission (722.6) introduced in 1996 is an outstanding unit, strong enough to be used on Mercedes' SLR McLaren sports car. Gearshifts should be smooth and responsive. In a change to its original

Early four-speed automatic transmission selector. (Courtesy Mercedes-Benz Classic)

service guidelines, Mercedes now recommends that the automatic transmission fluid be changed every 40,000 miles or 60,000km. 'Tired' or poor quality fluid can harm the electronic speed sensor plate inside the transmission, affecting the gear changes, so look for evidence of regular changes on the car you are buying. A seemingly minor leak from the transmission – from the electrical plug connector into the gearbox – is also important to catch early, as the fluid can make its way up to the ECU, causing serious damage.

The rare manual transmission is notchy, but generally tough; make sure that each gear engages cleanly and that the clutch is not slipping.

Suspension

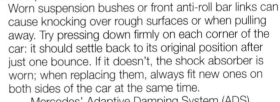

The R129's suspension was a big step forward from its predecessor, with a new strut-type suspension at the front and a sophisticated multi-link set-up at the rear. The weight of the SL is hard on the car though, and can cause suspension components such as the rear springs to crack.

At the front, check for worn top mounts, which will cause the car to wander.

Worn suspension bushes or front anti-roll bar links can cause knocking over rough surfaces or when pulling away. Try pressing down firmly on each corner of the car: it should settle back to its original position after just one bounce. If it doesn't, the shock absorber is worn; when replacing them, always fit new ones on both sides of the car at the same time.

Mercedes' Adaptive Damping System (ADS) was fitted as standard on the 600SL/SL600 and as an option on other models. Although even more comfortable than the standard steel suspension, it is a mixed blessing when buying secondhand. The complex electronic and hydraulic system can cause a range of problems, affecting the car's ride and handling. The pipes can corrode and leak, or the valve bodies fail. The plastic fluid level indicator for the hydraulic reservoir can snap and fall into the hydraulic

Front suspension top mounts – one of the points to check.

system, interfering with the hydraulic pumps. If the suspension seems to be rock hard, the Citroën-like accumulator spheres may be failing. The gas diaphragms at each wheel can split, making the car bounce unnecessarily. If a complete overhaul of an ADS system is required, you could be looking at a bill of ●x5000-10,000.

The regular suspension is a lot more straightforward, but converting an ADS-equipped car back to standard spec is a difficult job; getting the ride height right is particularly tricky.

Steering

The R129 remained faithful to the recirculating ball steering which Mercedes had long preferred. This lacks some precision compared to rack and pinion systems, but play should not be excessive. If it is, replacing the steering idler can help for a modest outlay. Changing a worn steering damper (only ●x40 from Mercedes) will also improve feel.

More modern design of steering wheel on final-generation cars. (Courtesy Mercedes-Benz Classic)

Tyres

For a heavy, high-performance car like the R129, it is essential to fit the best possible tyres, with the size, speed and load ratings recommended by Mercedes.

Check the dimensions, speed and load ratings for the tyres carefully.

Look for a premium brand, preferably of the same type front and rear. The tyres should have plenty of tread left (at least 4mm), and be no more than five years old, as rubber hardens over time and the tyres will perform less well. (See Chapter 15 for details of how to check the date of manufacture.)

Uneven tread wear is usually the result of poor alignment; a full geometry check will save you money in the long run, as well as restoring the car's handling. If you see wear on the inside of the rear tyres, this may be due to play in the rear trunnion bushes, which connect the lower suspension arm to the hub, and ultimately the car's handling will be affected. Fixing them needs a special tool, but is not an expensive job. On cars fitted with ADS, this may also be the first warning of problems in the hydraulic system.

Brakes

The SL's weight and performance make sure that its brakes – among the best available when the car was new – are given a good workout. Fortunately, they present no particular problems. Ask the seller when the pads and discs (rotors) were last changed, and look for signs of corrosion, ridges or

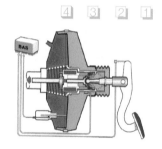

Mercedes introduced its Brake Assist System (BAS) in 1996. (Courtesy Mercedes-Benz Classic)

pitting on the discs. Juddering under heavy braking may mean that the discs are warped and will need to be replaced. If you can get underneath the car, check the condition of the rear brake hoses, which can perish.

Underbody

As well as the exhaust and suspension components mentioned already, getting the car on a lift or over an inspection pit is a great opportunity to assess its overall condition. If this is not possible on the seller's premises, you may be able to arrange it at a local workshop. Look for signs of rust on the sills, floorpan and chassis members, especially on cars which have regularly been driven in wet or snowy conditions. An application of underseal will help protect any car, but if it is very recent, be suspicious as it may be hiding corrosion or other damage. On the 600SL/SL600, check the oil sump too, as this can crack if the car grounds on a rough road.

An underbody inspection is essential on cars of this age. (Courtesy Turnbull & Oliver)

Professional inspection

Having your car inspected by a Mercedes specialist can often be a sound investment, giving you extra peace of mind when buying a good car … and maybe saving you from buying a 'bad 'un.' No genuine seller should object to this, provided of course that you cover any costs involved. It's worthwhile plugging the car into Mercedes' 'Star' diagnostic system and checking any fault codes which this generates: some may be quite benign,

Some official dealerships now have specialist 'Classic' departments.

while others will point to problems or repairs that need to be carried out. An official Mercedes-Benz dealer should also be able to tell you what recall work has been carried out on the car or remains outstanding.

Evaluation procedure

Add up the total points from each section.

Score: 112 = perfect; 84 = good; 56 = average; 28 = buyer beware! Cars scoring over 84 should be completely usable and require the minimum of repair or rectification, although continued service maintenance and care will be required to keep them in good condition. Cars scoring between 56 and 83 will require serious work (at much the same cost regardless of score). Cars scoring between 28 and 55 will require very careful assessment of the repair costs needed.

10 Auctions

– sold! Another way to buy your dream

Auction pros & cons

Pros: Prices are often lower than those of dealers or private sellers, and you might grab a real bargain on the day. Auctioneers have usually established clear title with the seller. At the venue, you can usually examine documentation relating to the vehicle.
Cons: You have to rely on a sketchy catalogue description of condition & history. The opportunity to inspect is limited and you cannot drive the car. Auction cars are often a little below par and may require some work. It's easy to overbid. There will usually be a buyer's premium to pay in addition to the auction hammer price.

Which auction?

Auctions by established auctioneers are advertised in car magazines and on the auction houses' websites. A catalogue, or a simple printed list of the lots for auctions might only be available a day or two ahead, though often lots are listed and pictured on auctioneers' websites much earlier. Contact the auction company to ask if previous auction selling prices are available, as this is useful information (details of past sales are often available on websites).

Catalogue, entry fee, and payment details

When you purchase the catalogue of vehicles in an auction, it often acts as a ticket allowing two people to attend the viewing days and the auction. Catalogue details tend to be comparatively brief, but will include information such as 'one owner from new, low mileage, full service history,' etc. It will also usually show a guide price to give you some idea of what to expect to pay, and will tell you what is charged as a 'buyer's premium.' The catalogue will also contain details of acceptable forms of payment. At the fall of the hammer an immediate deposit is usually required, the balance payable within 24 hours. If the plan is to pay by cash, there may be a cash limit. Some auctions will accept payment by debit card. Sometimes credit or charge cards are acceptable, but will often incur an extra charge. A bank draft or bank transfer will have to be arranged in advance with your own bank as well as with the auction house. No car will be released before *all* payments are cleared. If delays occur in payment transfers, then storage costs can accrue.

Buyer's premium

A buyer's premium will be added to the hammer price: *don't* forget this in your calculations. It is not usual for there to be a further state tax or local tax on the purchase price and/or on the buyer's premium.

Viewing

In some instances, it's possible to view on the day, or days before, as well as in the hours prior to, the auction. There are auction officials available who are willing to help out by opening engine and luggage compartments and to allow you to inspect the interior. While the officials may start the engine for you, a test drive is out of the question. Crawling under and around the car as much as you want is permitted, but you can't suggest that the car you are interested in be jacked up, or attempt to do the job yourself. You can also ask to see any documentation available.

Bidding

Before you take part in the auction, decide your maximum bid – and stick to it!

It may take a while for the auctioneer to reach the lot you are interested in, so use that time to observe how other bidders behave. When it's the turn of your car, attract the auctioneer's attention and make an early bid. The auctioneer will then look to you for a reaction every time another bid is made, usually the bids will be in fixed increments until the bidding slows, when smaller increments will often be accepted before the hammer falls. If you want to withdraw from the bidding, make sure the auctioneer understands your intentions – a vigorous shake of the head when he or she looks to you for the next bid should do the trick!

Assuming that you are the successful bidder, the auctioneer will note your card or paddle number, and from that moment on you will be responsible for the vehicle.

If the car is unsold, either because it failed to reach the reserve or because there was little interest, it may be possible to negotiate with the owner, via the auctioneers, after the sale is over.

Successful bid

There are two more items to think about. How to get the car home, and insurance. If you can't drive the car, your own or a hired trailer is one way, another is to have the vehicle shipped using the facilities of a local company. The auction house will also have details of companies specialising in the transfer of cars.

Insurance for immediate cover can usually be purchased on site, but it may be more cost-effective to make arrangements with your own insurance company in advance, and then call to confirm the full details.

eBay & other online auctions

eBay & other online auctions could land you a car at a bargain price, though you'd be foolhardy to bid without examining the car first, something most vendors encourage. A useful feature of eBay is that the geographical location of the car is shown, so you can narrow your choices to those within a realistic radius of home. Be prepared to be outbid in the last few moments of the auction. Remember, your bid is binding and that it will be very, very difficult to get restitution in the case of a crooked vendor fleecing you – *caveat emptor!*

Be aware that some cars offered for sale in online auctions are 'ghost' cars. *Don't* part with *any* cash without being sure that the vehicle does actually exist and is as described (usually pre-bidding inspection is possible).

Auctioneers

Barrett-Jackson www.barrett-jackson.com/
Bonhams www.bonhams.com/
Coys www.coys.co.uk/
eBay www.eBay.com/
H&H www.handh.co.uk/
RM www.rmsothebys.com/
Shannons www.shannons.com.au/
Silver www.silverauctions.com/

11 Paperwork
– correct documentation is essential!

The paper trail
Enthusiasts' cars often come with a large portfolio of paperwork accumulated by a succession of proud owners. This documentation represents the real history of the car, and shows the level of care the car has received, how it's been used, which specialists have worked on it, and the dates of major repairs. The prices of early R129s have now fallen to a point where some owners may be able to afford to buy the car, but won't have enough spare cash to replace some parts, the prices for which still match the cost of the cars when new; finding an SL with a comprehensive history file is already a great start. Be especially wary of cars with little paperwork to support claims of major work.

Registration documents
All countries/states have some form of registration for private vehicles, whether it's like the American 'pink slip' system or the British 'log book' system.

It is essential to check that the registration document is genuine, that it relates to the car in question, and that all the vehicle's details are correctly recorded, including chassis/VIN and engine numbers (if these are shown). If you are buying from the previous owner, his or her name and address will be recorded in the document; this will not be the case if you are buying from a dealer.

In the UK, the current registration document is named 'V5C,' and is printed in coloured sections of blue, green and pink. The blue section relates to the car specification, the green section has details of the new owner and the pink section is sent to the DVLA in the UK when the car is sold. A small section in yellow deals with selling the car within the motor trade.

In the UK, the DVLA will provide details of earlier keepers of the vehicle upon payment of a small fee, and much can be learned in this way.

If the car has a foreign registration, there may be expensive and time-consuming formalities to complete. Do you really want the hassle?

Roadworthiness certificate
Most country/state administrations require that vehicles are regularly tested to prove that they are safe to use on the public highway and do not produce excessive emissions. In the UK that test (the 'MoT') is carried out at approved testing stations, for a fee. In the USA the requirement varies, but most states insist on an emissions test every two years as a minimum, while the police are charged with pulling over unsafe-looking vehicles.

In the UK, the test is required on an annual basis once a vehicle becomes three years old. Of particular relevance for older cars is that the certificate issued includes the mileage reading recorded at the test date and, therefore, becomes an independent record of that car's history. Ask the seller if previous certificates are available. Without an MoT, the vehicle should be trailered to its new home, unless you insist that a valid MoT is part of the deal. (Not such a bad idea this, as at least you will know the car was roadworthy on the day it was tested, and you don't need to wait for the old certificate to expire before having the test done.)

In the UK, vehicles over 40 years old on May 20th each year, are exempt from MOT testing. Owners can still have the test carried out if they so wish.

Road licence

The administration of every country/state charges some kind of tax for the use of its road system, the actual form of the 'road licence' and, how it is displayed, varying enormously country to country and state to state.

Whatever the form of the road licence, it must relate to the vehicle carrying it and must be present and valid if the car is to be driven on the public highway legally.

Changed legislation in the UK means that the seller of a car must surrender any existing road fund licence, and it is the responsibility of the new owner to re-tax the vehicle at the time of purchase and before the car can be driven on the road. It's therefore vital to see the Vehicle Registration Certificate (V5C) at the time of purchase, and to have access to the New Keeper Supplement (V5C/2), allowing the buyer to obtain road tax immediately.

In the UK, classic vehicles 40 years old or more on the 1st January each year get free road tax. It is still necessary to renew the tax status every year, even if there is no change.

If the car is untaxed because it has not been used for a period of time, the owner has to inform the licensing authorities.

Valuation certificate

A private vendor may have a recent valuation certificate, or letter signed by a recognised expert stating how much he, or she, believes the particular car to be worth (such documents, together with photos, are usually needed to get 'agreed value' insurance). Generally, such documents should act only as confirmation of your own assessment of the car rather than a guarantee of value. The easiest way to find out how to obtain a formal valuation is to contact the owners' club.

Data cards and VIN

Each Mercedes left the factory with a detailed data card, describing the exact model, colour and trim, and the codes for each option fitted. These codes – which you can look up on many online sites – should

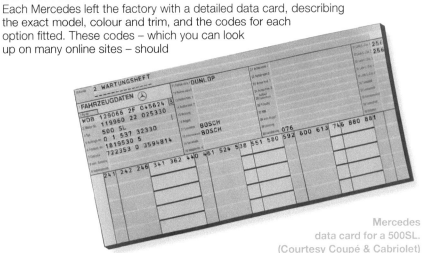

Mercedes
data card for a 500SL.
(Courtesy Coupé & Cabriolet)

correspond to the actual equipment on the car you are viewing, and provide valuable confirmation of its authenticity. If the card is missing, Mercedes-Benz' Classic department in your country may be able to supply a replacement.

The 17-digit VIN (Vehicle Identification Number) on the card should tally with that on the car, which you can find inside the driver's door jamb and in the engine compartment. It may also be etched on the windows as a security measure.

For the earliest R129s with a Becker radio, you should also find a safety code card with the re-set code to be used in an emergency.

VIN sticker in driver's door jamb.

Code card for early Becker radio.

Service history

Try to obtain as much service history and other paperwork pertaining to the car as you can. Naturally, dealer stamps, or specialist garage receipts score most points in the value stakes. However, anything helps in the great authenticity game: items such as the original bill of sale, handbook, parts invoices and repair bills adding to the story and the character of the car. Even a brochure correct to the year of the car's manufacture is a useful document and something that you could well have to search hard to locate in future years. If the seller claims that the car has been restored, then expect receipts and other evidence from a specialist restorer.

If the seller claims to have carried out regular servicing at home, ask what work was completed, when, and seek some evidence of it being carried out. Your assessment of the car's overall condition should tell you whether the seller's claims are genuine.

Restoration photographs

Most R129s are still too new to have undergone a complete restoration, but you may find cars which have received major bodywork repairs after an accident. If the seller tells you that the car has undergone significant work, ask to be shown a series of photographs taken while the work was under way. These should help you gauge the thoroughness of the work. If you buy the car, ask if you can have all the photographs, as they form an important part of the vehicle's history. It's surprising how many sellers are happy to part with their car and accept your cash, but want to hang on to their photographs! In the latter event, you may be able to persuade the vendor to get a set of copies made.

12 What's it worth?

– let your head rule your heart!

Condition

If the car you've been looking at is really bad, then you've probably not bothered to use the marking system in Chapter 9: 60-minute evaluation. You may not have even got as far as using that chapter at all!

If you did use the marking system in Chapter 9, you'll know whether the car is in Excellent (maybe Concours), Good, Average or Poor condition or, perhaps, somewhere in-between these categories.

Many enthusiasts' car magazines run a regular price guide. If you haven't bought the latest editions, do so now and compare their suggested values for the model you are thinking of buying; also look at the auction prices they're reporting. The values published in the magazines tend to vary from one magazine to another, as do their scales of condition, so read carefully the guidance notes they provide. Bear in mind that a car that is truly a recent show winner could be worth more than the highest scale published. Assuming that the car you have in mind is not in show/concours condition, then relate the level of condition that you judge the car to be in with the appropriate guide price. How does the figure compare with the asking price? Before you start haggling with the seller, consider what effect any variation from standard specification might have on the car's value. If you are buying from a dealer, remember there will be a dealer's premium on the price.

Prices for the R129 generation of SLs have already bottomed out; values of cars in good condition, with a full service history, are starting to climb. At the time of writing, cars on sale in continental Europe offer no savings over cars in the UK, and will come with left-hand drive. Forecasting the market for emerging classics is always hard, but there is every chance that an R129 bought today will at the very least hold its value, and that prices of the most desirable cars will increase over time.

Desirable options/extras

As the R129 gains classic status, originality is becoming increasingly important and should be considered essential if you are buying with an eye on future investment potential.

Brochure shot of the panoramic hardtop. (Courtesy Mercedes-Benz Classic)

Dark metallic colours suit the SL well. (Courtesy Turnbull & Oliver)

The R129 was increasingly well equipped during its lifecycle, and nearly all cars for sale will have automatic transmission, leather upholstery, and fully automatic air-conditioning. On second- and third-generation cars, the panoramic hardtop is highly sought-after. The seals for this are different from the earlier standard hardtop, so retro-fitting one is a big job.

One of several styles of AMG wheel offered over the years.

AMG wheels (on non-AMG models) are a matter of taste, but are probably the only accessory wheels worth considering.

The R129 looks good in most dark colours, including black and dark blue metallic (especially classy with a light cream interior). Silver is also a classic choice, whilst red sold well in the US.

Undesirable features

Cars with manual transmission and cloth interiors are extremely rare outside Germany, and will be hard to sell on. Some colours which were popular in Germany, including Beryl (turquoise) and Impala (brown), can be more difficult to sell in other markets. The Burgundy leather upholstery which Mercedes-Benz used for many of its launch cars is also an acquired taste today.

All but a handful of German-market cars came as standard with a hardtop, and this is costly to replace, so don't be fobbed off with any excuses if the car you are viewing has a soft top only. The windstop became standard in 1993, but this is relatively inexpensive to replace if missing.

Red cloth interior – a hard sell today. (Courtesy Mercedes-Benz Classic)

Unless they are from top-end specialists such as AMG, Brabus and Carlsson, aftermarket modifications and accessories are best avoided. Large non-standard wheels can put extra stress on suspension components, whilst non-original stereos, satellite navigation systems and alarms can cause electrical problems.

Striking a deal

Negotiate on the basis of your condition assessment, mileage, and fault rectification cost. Also take into account the car's specification. Be realistic about the value, but don't be completely intractable: a small compromise on the part of the vendor or buyer will often facilitate a deal at little real cost.

13 Do you really want to restore?

– it'll take longer and cost more than you think

For some enthusiasts, restoring a car is just as rewarding, if not more so, than actually owning and driving it. For them, nothing will beat the peace of mind that comes from knowing how each part was refurbished and re-assembled.

For the R129 SL, it is too early for a full-scale restoration to make sense, for two main reasons. First, with over 200,000 SLs sold new and Mercedes-Benz' traditional high build quality, there are still a great many cars to choose from, from throughout its lifecycle and in each mechanical specification. You will almost certainly find the right car if you spend some more time searching. Local clubs can often help you find good cars, as can extending your search to other parts of the country or neighbouring states. The time and money you invest now is certain to be a fraction of what you might spend putting right a car in poor condition. Why not buy a good car now and enjoy driving it straightaway?

The second reason is that any classic Mercedes is likely to be an expensive car to restore. As we have seen, many service items are readily available at moderate prices. Major mechanical components, however, are another thing altogether. A full engine and transmission rebuild could well cost more than the value of the car. The 600SL/SL600, with duplicate parts like the wiring harness for each bank of its twelve-cylinder engine, will be particularly expensive to overhaul. Any car with the sophisticated Adaptive Damping System (ADS) will also be costly to refurbish. Trim parts can also be eye-wateringly expensive; other parts may need to be made up specially. The R129 is a complex car, with sophisticated mechanical and electronic components: working on it often needs specialist tools and a high level of expertise, which only professional restorers can provide. With parts prices like these, and the labour rates charged by specialists, completely restoring an R129 simply isn't an economic proposition today. That may change one day, but it is too soon to know whether values of the R129 will spiral upwards in the same way as the 190SL or the 'Pagoda' models which went before it.

You may find some cars which have suffered accident damage and where the repairs would be too expensive for an insurance company to approve, but which can be purchased very cheaply and returned to roadworthy condition. Here again it's unlikely that you will recoup your costs: potential buyers will always be apprehensive when you come to sell on cars like these.

Not for the faint-hearted!

14 Paint problems
– bad complexion, including dimples, pimples and bubbles

Paint faults generally occur due lack of protection/maintenance, or to poor preparation prior to a respray or touch-up. Some of the following conditions may be present in the car you're looking at:

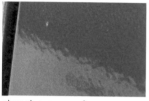

Orange peel

This appears as an uneven paint surface, similar to the skin of an orange. This fault is caused by the failure of atomized paint droplets to flow into each other when they hit the surface. It's sometimes possible to rub out the effect with proprietary paint cutting/rubbing compound or very fine grades of abrasive paper. A respray may be necessary in severe cases. Consult a bodywork repairer/paint shop for advice on the particular car.

Cracking

Severe cases are likely to have been caused by too heavy an application of paint (or filler beneath the paint). Also, insufficient stirring of the paint before application can lead to the components being improperly mixed, and cracking can result. Incompatibility with the paint already on the panel can have a similar effect. To rectify the problem, it is necessary to rub down to a smooth, sound finish before respraying the problem area.

Crazing

Sometimes the paint takes on a crazed rather than a cracked appearance when the problems mentioned under 'Cracking' are present. This problem can also be caused by a reaction between the underlying surface and the paint. Paint removal and respraying the problem area is usually the only solution.

Blistering

Almost always caused by corrosion of the metal beneath the paint. Usually perforation will be found in the metal and the damage will usually be worse than that suggested by the area of blistering. The metal will have to be repaired before repainting.

In 1993, Mercedes moved to water-based paints, which caused corrosion problems on some of its cars, but the R129 was less affected than models such as the W124 series.

Micro blistering

Usually the result of an economy respray where inadequate heating has allowed moisture to settle on the car before spraying. Consult a paint specialist, but usually damaged paint will have to be removed before partial or full respraying. Can also be caused by car covers that don't 'breathe.'

Fading

Some colours, especially reds, are prone to fading if subjected to strong sunlight for long periods without the benefit of polish protection. Sometimes proprietary paint restorers and/or paint cutting/rubbing compounds will retrieve the situation. Often a respray is the only real solution.

Many SLs were sold in dark metallic finishes. (Courtesy Turnbull & Oliver)

Peeling

Often a problem with metallic paintwork when the sealing lacquer becomes damaged and begins to peel off. Poorly applied paint may also peel. The remedy is to strip and start again!

Dimples

Dimples in the paintwork are caused by the residue of polish (particularly silicone types) not being removed properly before respraying. Paint removal and repainting is the only solution.

Dents

Small dents are usually easily cured by the 'Dentmaster' or equivalent process, that sucks or pushes out the dent (as long as the paint surface is still intact). Companies offering dent removal services usually come to your home; consult your telephone directory or search online.

Red paint can fade in strong sunlight. (Courtesy Mercedes-Benz Classic)

15 Problems due to lack of use

– just like their owners, SLs need exercise!

Many Mercedes convertibles are used as second or third cars and may go for long periods without being run, which does them no favours.

Seized and rusted components

Pistons in callipers, slave and master cylinders can seize.
The foot-operated parking brake can seize, if the cables and linkages rust.

Fluids

All fluids should be replaced at regular intervals, and the air-conditioning recharged. Good quality coolant is essential to avoid premature corrosion of the aluminium components in the engine, cooling and heating system, and to avoid the risk of serious damage. Silt settling and solidifying can result in overheating.

Brake fluid absorbs water from the atmosphere and should be renewed every two years.

Check the DOT code on each tyre.

Tyre problems

Tyres that have had the weight of the car on them in a single position for some time will develop flat spots, resulting in some (usually temporary) vibration. The tyre walls may have cracks or (blister-type) bulges, meaning new tyres are needed. Even if the tyres appear to be in good condition, check the DOT code on the sidewall, which will show you the week and year of manufacture. The tyre in the photo is from week 32 of 2006. At more than 15 years old, the tread compound will have hardened and the performance of the tyre will be affected.

Shock absorbers (dampers)

With lack of use, the dampers will lose their elasticity or even seize. Creaking, groaning and stiff suspension are signs of this problem.

For cars fitted with the Adaptive Damping System (ADS), the system should be used regularly in all its different modes (including the front-end lift facility), to keep it working smoothly.

Rubber and plastic

Radiator hoses may have perished and split, possibly resulting in the loss of all coolant. Window, door and rear light seals can all harden and leak. Gaiters and boots can crack. Wiper blades will harden.

The hood mechanism should be used regularly, or creases can form and the plastic window sections may be damaged. This will also help the mechanism itself operate correctly.

Interior trim

The leather trim in the car needs regular conditioning (every six months) if it is to stay supple and in good condition. Cars left in the sun can suffer from dried or cracked dashboards and other trim.

Electrics

The battery will be of little use if it has not been charged for many months. If a car is left standing for several weeks, connecting it to a trickle charger will keep it in good condition. It is essential not to jump-start an R129 with a flat battery: the spike in voltage can fry the ECU for the hood mechanism – and the replacement part costs ●x1700 (without labour)!

Earthing/grounding problems are common when the connections have corroded. Wiring insulation can harden and fail.

The battery is located in the boot (trunk).

Rotting exhaust system

Exhaust gas contains a high water content, so exhaust systems corrode very quickly from the inside when the car is not used. This even applies to stainless steel systems.

16 The Community

– key people, organisations and companies in the R129 world

Owners of the R129-series SLs will find plenty of organisations and individuals ready to help them look after their cars.

Clubs

Mercedes-Benz lends its support to more than 80 independent clubs worldwide, and many of these have model registers dedicated to the R129. Benefits available to members include technical information, discounted services such as insurance, professionally produced club magazines and the chance to join frequent social and driving events. You can find out more at:

- Mercedes-Benz Classic (factory homepage): https://www.mercedes-benz.com/en/classic/
- UK: https://mercedes-benz-club.co.uk/
- North America: www.mbca.org

Specialists

Expertise in maintaining the R129 is gradually disappearing from the official dealer network, but plenty of independent specialists are stepping up. As the R129's status as an upcoming classic is recognised, new companies are beginning to specialise in it, alongside established dealers and workshops handling all classic Mercedes.

In North America, it's worth starting with one of the 85 local sections of the club, which should be able to recommend a dealer or workshop near you.

In the UK, dealers such as these often have a good selection of R129s for sale and can help look after your car:

- Avantgarde Classics (Staffordshire): https://www.avantgardeclassics.co.uk/
- Charles Ironside (Hampshire): www.charlesironside.co.uk
- Cheshire Classic Benz: www.ccbenz.co.uk
- Edward Hall (Buckinghamshire): www.edward-hall.co.uk
- The SL Shop (Worcestershire): www.theslshop.com
- Turnbull & Oliver (Hampshire): www.usedmercedesbenz-sales.co.uk

A noted British specialist in hood and interior repairs is d:class, based in Surrey (www.dclass.co.uk). You will find advertisements for many other companies in the magazines listed below.

Parts and accessories

Many service parts remain available from your local Mercedes dealer, but prices can sometimes be high, and you may prefer to order online from a specialist parts supplier such as these:

- UK – Mercedes Parts Centre: mercedes-parts-centre.co.uk and PFS Parts: www.partsformercedes-benz.com
- USA – Pelican Parts: www.pelicanparts.com/catalog/SuperCat/R129_catalog.htm

Useful sources of information

Three English-language magazines cater to classic Mercedes enthusiasts and often feature the R129:

- *Mercedes Enthusiast* (monthly) and *Classic Mercedes* (quarterly) can be found at large newsstands in both the UK and North America, or obtained on subscription from www.mercedesenthusiast.co.uk and https://www.classicmercedesmagazine.com respectively.
- *Mercedes-Benz Classic* is published in English and German by Mercedes itself, twice a year: subscribe at www.mercedes-benz.com/en/mercedes-benz/lifestyle/mercedes-benz-magazines/classic-magazine/subscription/

As well as Mercedes-Benz' own manuals and technical literature, there are plenty of books for enthusiasts to read up on the R129-series SL. Brian Long's comprehensive history of the model, *Mercedes-Benz SL R129-series 1989-2001*, from Veloce Publishing (www.veloce.co.uk) can be particularly recommended. Brooklands Books (www.brooklandsbooks.co.uk) devotes one of its excellent compilations of period road tests to the pre-facelift cars: *Mercedes SLs Performance Portfolio 1989-1994*.

If you speak German, there is even more information available online at www.r129sl-club.de and www.129sl-forum.de.

Mercedes' SL heritage on show at Retro Classics, Stuttgart.

17 Vital statistics

– essential data at your fingertips

Production figures

Model	Production period: pre-production to end	Number of units
300SL	1988-1993	12,020
300SL-24	1988-1993	26,984
SL280	1993-1998	10,319
SL280 (V6)	1997-2001	1704
SL320	1993-1998	32,223
SL320 (V6)	1997-2001	7070
500SL/SL500	1988-1998	79,827
SL500 (M113 engine)	1997-2001	23,704
600SL/SL600	1991-2001	11,089
Total		**204,940**

Production figures for the AMG versions are not documented separately by Mercedes, but are estimated at under 1000 units; more than half of these the SL60 model.

Technical specifications
Engine and transmission

Model	Engine capacity (cc)	Engine type	Cylinders & layout	Peak power (bhp) at rpm	Maximum torque (lb/ft) at rpm	Transmissions available
300SL	3000	M103 E00	Straight-six	190/5700	192/4300	5M/4A
300SL-24	2960	M104 E30	Straight-six	231/5500	201/4600	5M/4A or 5A
SL280	2799	M104 E28	Straight-six	193/5500	199/3750	5M/4A or 5A
SL280 (V6)	2799	M112 E28	V6	204/5700	199/3000-5000	5M/5A
SL320	3199	M104 E32	Straight-six	231/5600	232/3750	5A
SL320 (V6)	3199	M112 E32	V6	224/5600	232/3000-4800	5A
500SL/SL500 (first generation)	4973	M119 E50	V8	326/5500	332/4000	4A
SL500 (third generation)	4966	M113 E50	V8	306/5600	339/2700-4250	5A
600SL/SL600	5987	M120 E60	V12	394/5200	420/3800	4A, then 5A
SL60 AMG	5958	M119 E60	V8	381/5500	428/3750	4A, then 5A

Running gear

Independent suspension all-round, with MacPherson struts at front and five-link rear suspension. Available Adaptive Damping System (ADS).

Steering by recirculating ball, with standard power assistance.

Four-wheel disc brakes, ventilated at front on all years and at rear from July 1993, with ABS as standard. Brake Assist System (BAS) from December 1996.

Wheel sizes progressively increased during production, from 16in at launch to 18in on late AMG models. Tyre sizes followed suit, ranging from 225/55 ZR16 on first cars to 275/35 ZR18 (at rear) on AMG versions.

Performance figures

Model	Top speed	Acceleration: 0-100km/h (62mph) in seconds
300SL	139mph (223km/h)	9.5
300SL-24	146mph (235km/h)	8.4
SL280	140mph (225km/h)	9.9
SL280 (V6)	142mph (228km/h)	9.5
SL320	149mph (240km/h)	8.4
SL320 (V6)	148mph (238km/h)	8.4
500SL/SL500	155mph (250km/h)	6.5
SL500 (M113 engine from 1997)	155mph (250km/h)	6.5
600SL/SL600	155mph (250km/h)	6.1
SL60 AMG	155mph (250km/h)	5.6

All figures are for cars fitted with automatic transmission and as quoted by Marco Ruiz, *Mercedes-Benz 1991-2001* (Opera Omnia).

Dimensions

All models	First generation	Second and third generations
Length	4470mm (176.0in)	4499mm (177.1in)
Width	1812mm (71.3in)	
Height (with hardtop)	1307mm (51.5in)	1303mm (51.3in)
Wheelbase	2515mm (99.0in)	
Fuel tank (all models)	80 litres (21.1 USgal)	
Luggage capacity	265 litres/9.35 cubic feet	

Weight

Varies widely by model, engine size and standard equipment fitted, but no R129 is a lightweight! As a guide:

First-generation 300SL: 1650kg (3638lb)
Third-generation SL600: 2050kg (4519lb).

Also from Veloce Publishing –

MERCEDES-BENZ
SL R129 series

1989 to 2001

Brian Long

This detailed and beautifully illustrated book covers the Mercedes-Benz 129-series, which ran from 1989 to 2001. Written by a respected motoring writer, with many years' ownership of the Mercedes SL models behind him, this will no-doubt prove to be the definitive study of the subject. All major markets are looked at, giving a true picture of what was available, where and when. Extensive appendices cover engine specifications, chassis numbers, build numbers, and much more.

ISBN: 978-1-845844-48-6
Hardback • 25x25cm • 208 pages • 370 colour and b&w pictures

For more info on Veloce titles, visit our website at www.veloce.co.uk • email: info@ veloce.co.uk • Tel: +44(0)1305 260068

MERCEDES-BENZ
SLK R171 series

2004-2011

Brian Long

This book reveals the full history of the second generation Mercedes-Benz SLK, covering in detail the German, US, UK, Australian and Japanese markets. The perfect book to grace a Mercedes-Benz enthusiasts' library shelf, it's the definitive record of the model illustrated with stunning photographs.

ISBN: 978-1-845846-53-4
Hardback • 24.8x24.8cm • 224 pages • 388 colour pictures

For more info on Veloce titles, visit our website at www.veloce.co.uk • email: info@veloce.co.uk • Tel: +44(0)1305 260068

The Essential Buyer's Guide™ series ...

For more details visit:
www.veloce.co.uk
email: info@veloce.co.uk
tel: 01305 260068

Index